The
SPUR BOOK
of
YOUTH HOSTELLING

The
SPUR BOOK
of
YOUTH HOSTELLING

Cameron McNeish

SPURBOOKS LIMITED

Published by:
SPURBOOKS LTD.
6 Parade Court
Bourne End
Buckinghamshire

ISBN 0 904978 98 2

Printed by Maund & Irvine Ltd., Tring, Herts.

CONTENTS

INTRODUCTION

ABOUT THIS SERIES

Venture Guides are designed as basic guides for outdoor people and fall into two broad areas.

The first group covers skills, and includes such subjects as Knot tying and Splicing, Map and Compass work, Camping and Cooking skills, Weather Lore, First Aid, and Survival and Rescue techniques.

The second group covers what we describe as Venture Sports, which are activities requiring little mechanical assistance, and are not team games. This group includes such subjects as Backpacking and Hilltrekking, Sailing, Dinghy Cruising, Cross-Country and Downhill Skiing, Walking, Camping, and now, the subject of this book, Youth Hostelling.

ABOUT THIS BOOK

Cameron McNeish, the author of this book, is Hostel Warden at Aviemore in the Cairngorms, an experienced outdoorsman and a well-known writer on outdoor affairs.

He has written two other books on the outdoors *Highland Ways*, and the Spurbook Master Guide, *Snow Camping*, and has regular features in all the outdoor magazines.

In this book he describes and illustrates the whole scope of youth hostelling in the UK and overseas, and shows how to get the very most from all hostel based outdoor activities.

FIGURE 1

Chapter 1

THE YOUTH HOSTEL MOVEMENT

Today, within the United Kingdom, more and more people, particularly young people, are feeling the need to escape from the pressures of their everyday lives, and leisure activities are booming as they have never done before. For the first time in the country's history, statistics show that there are more people now actively participating in sport, than there are spectating. Perhaps this is because of the increased leisure time available nowadays, or perhaps it is because more and more people are appreciating the benefits of regular exercise thanks to extensive propaganda from the Home Office and Health Service.

Whatever the reason, there is no doubt that much of this exercise is being taken in Britain's countryside; in the mountains and on our lakes and rivers, and even in the quiet byways of our rural countryside. This is all very nice for those who can afford to travel every weekend from their home in the city to the countryside and stay in a hotel or guest house. It is also fine for those who can afford the initial outlay for camping equipment.

But what about the large numbers who cannot possibly afford the luxuries of a hotel, or those who could not hope to raise the necessary cash for a complete camping kit, those who have to live on a university grant, or young people still at school who have no real income to speak of at all? Then there are the older folk, many with young families, who are saving like mad to pay off a mortgage and have difficulty saving for a holiday as well. Are these people to be denied the pleasures of the countryside, simply for lack of somewhere to stay? Thanks to a man called Richard Schirrmann, the answer is no.

IDEALS

In 1929, Schirrmann, a German schoolteacher, took a party of schoolboys to an unused schoolhouse for their summer vacation, and the foundations of the Youth Hostel movement were laid. Schirrmann believed that young people should have some form of cheap, simple accommodation available scattered throughout the countryside, enabling them to travel and see something of the world, and not only in the countryside, but also in places of historic and cultural interest; places where they could find a clean bed at the end of a hard days travelling; where they could cook a meal and enjoy the company of others with similar interests.

The result of these beliefs is today a huge international movement with over 4,000 Youth Hostels in nearly fifty countries in places as widespread as Sri Lanka and Thailand, and from Japan to Uruguay.

OBJECTS

The chief object of the Youth Hostel movement of today is basically the same as Shirrmann's. To help all, but especially young people of limited means living and working in industrial and other areas, to know, use, and appreciate the countryside and places of historic and cultural interest, and to promote their health, recreation, and education particularly by providing simple hostel accommodation for them on their travels.

WHO USES HOSTELS?

What has changed quite significantly since the early days of youth hostelling are the types of people who come. No longer is it only the young people of limited means, but we find nowadays all types and ages of people hostelling. Couples who have hostelled in their younger days come back with their children, older folk who have hostelled since the very beginning and can't get out of the habit; in hostel car parks the occasional Jaguar and sports car mixes with the old bangers and push-bikes; school and universities send parties on educational excursions. The simple answer is that anyone can use a youth hostel, provided he or she is over five years of age and holds a current membership card which can be obtained from the Youth Hostel Association of his or her country. Race, creed or political beliefs have no bearing on membership.

THE ATTRACTION OF YOUTH HOSTELS

Why do people come to youth hostels, especially those who can afford the comfortable surroundings of a hotel? I think the answer lies in companionship and friendliness. Despite the fact that there are certain rules and regulations within the hostel framework, there is always a happy relaxed atmosphere in a hostel. Hostellers tend to mix very well together because they tend to have similar interests, whether they be walkers, climbers, cyclists, hitch-hikers or whatever. So often one sees a hotel lounge where the guests sit during the evening with hardly a word to say to one another. A youth hostel common room is so different. It buzzes with conversation and joviality. It never fails to surprise me when a dozen or so individual hostellers book in at the desk and within an hour or so they are all laughing and chatting with one another as though they had known each other all their lives. And it does not matter whether they be Greek, Japanese, Australian, or Dutch, the language barrier is soon surmounted and they will be busy explaining in sign language or broken English how they climbed such and such a hill, how they hitched a super lift in a Bentley, or where they are travelling to next day.

ORGANISATION
Another good factor is that the Youth Hostel Associations are run by hostellers, for hostellers. Paid staff is kept to a minimum, and regional and national committees are formed to deal with the running of the Association. No one is out to make a profit. When you become a member it is your Association, they are your youth hostels, and you help to make the rules and regulations for the benefit of everyone concerned, while you, and others like you, run the whole show.

Of course the other side of the 'do it yourself' idea is in the form of hostel duties. As there is no paid cleaning staff, the members lend a hand every day with the various hostel chores, cleaning, sweeping, chopping wood for the hostel fire, under the direction of the warden. This system not only keeps down running costs and therefore bednight charges, but it helps foster an interest in the hostel itself, and helps encourage a co-operative spirit so important when people have to live together in harmony.

THE HOSTELS
Many of the hostels themselves are of considerable interest and well worth a visit in their own right. They range from modern purpose-built buildings to very old castles, from farm houses to mansions, from shepherds huts to water-mills. All provide dormitory accommodation, with separate dorms for men and women of course, washing facilities, mostly with showers, a common room where you can relax after a hard day and a kitchen where members can cook their own meals. Many hostels also provide cooked meals prepared by the warden, but I think that self-cooking encourages independence, and many friends can be made while exchanging meals and menus over the hostel stove.

In the smaller hostels, the kitchen is the main meeting place and social point. Along the shelves are rows of shining kettles and pans. Below the ceiling, anoraks, socks and other items are draped over drying lines. Underneath is the stove round which the hostellers are milling, flushed with the days activities and enjoying the relaxed open company; the stove is indeed the focal

11

point. Pots of various delicacies from chow mein to baked beans simmer away merrily, giving off aromas that make your mouth water. The whole atmosphere is friendly and cosy, and you feel at home instantly, even if you are a complete stranger.

GRADES
In the United Kingdom the hostels are graded and priced according to the facilities offered. The higher the grade, the more it costs per night. As the hostels are intended for active outdoor people, they are closed during the day, normally from 10 a.m. to 5 p.m., except in bad weather, when the warden will keep the doors open.

HOSTELLING GROUPS
Low charges and unpretentious facilities are the keys of the youth hostel movement. Although todays youngsters are somewhat more sophisticated than in the time of Richard Schirrmann, rising bednight figures prove that this combination is a successful one. But the future success of the movement depends on the active interest of its members. Local hostelling groups operate all over the country, and hold regular social events as well as weekend hostelling trips. Local groups come in all shapes and sizes. Some have well organised, comprehensive programmes, while others are run more informally, but one thing is certain, all will give the newcomer a warm welcome. Many local group members serve on regional and national committees, and as in other activities, find that putting back something into the hostelling movement increases the enjoyment they get back from it.

HOSTEL STAMPS
In the morning, once you have had your breakfast and completed your hostel duty, you collect your membership card from the warden. He will stamp the card with the hostel stamp to help you keep a record of your hostel visits. Each hostel has its own personalised stamp, many having very attractive designs. These stamps will form a happy record of your hostelling from your first tentative trip, through the years until the time comes when you introduce your own family to the delights of Youth Hostelling. Who knows, you may someday arrive at the hostel door with your grandchildren, on their first exploratory visit.

Many members' cards contain nostalgic memories of hostels now closed, and they can look back through the pages of stamps and recall many happy memories of their early hostelling years.

12

AVIEMORE

- 2 MAR 1978

EDINBURGH

BRUNTSFIELD
- 1 MAR 1978

New blanks for stamping obtainable from hostels

FIGURE 2

Chapter 2

RULES AND REGULATIONS

Although the title of this chapter may sound rather forbidding, rules and regulations are a necessary part of any large organisation. Youth Hostel rules have been drawn up by hostellers for hostellers, and are the results of many years experience. Compliance with the rules enables everyone to live together in a harmonious atmosphere, and adds to the comfort and enjoyment of all.

HOSTEL DUTIES

The main difference between staying in a youth hostel and living in other forms of accommodation, is that hostellers are given the opportunity to participate in the running of the hostel. Charges are kept as low as possible, and to help achieve this, everyone is expected to assist the warden in the simple domestic chores before they leave for the day. These chores, or hostel duties, which seldom take more than ten minutes, are allocated every morning by the warden, and consist of sweeping floors, cleaning windows, peeling potatoes, or chopping wood for the fire; it all helps the warden to keep a clean and tidy hostel. The hostel duty is a tradition, and everybody does something.

MEMBERSHIP CARD

Everyone who stays at a Youth Hostel must be a member of one of the fifty or so countries belonging to the International Youth Hostel Federation, and must be in possession of a current membership card. This card should be signed by the holder and is not transferable. This means that you are not allowed to lend it to Fred next door so that he may sample hostelling without becoming a member himself. The only exception to this rule is for those people under the charge of a Leader Card Holder. Leader Cards are issued to encourage the use of hostels by school and youth groups. The idea is to cut out the formality and expenditure of membership for the youngsters in such parties, provided they are under the control of a responsible adult leader. Leader Cards are issued to teachers and leaders of youth organisations who are members of the Youth Hostel Association of their own country.

ON ARRIVAL

Hand your membership card to the warden, sign your name and address in the hostel register, and pay the appropriate charges.

FOOTWEAR

Hiking and mountaineering boots must be removed before entering the hostel. So should Wellington boots, nailed footwear, and metal plated cycling shoes. These types of footwear can damage floors, and I'm sure you can visualise the effect a hundred pairs of vibram-soles a day can have on a lino floor. Many hostels still bear the scars of the stilleto-heel fashion of the Fifties and early Sixties in the form of pock-marked floors. So, remember, a little common sense goes a long way, and clean shiny floors can remain clean and shiny if everyone takes off his or her outdoor footwear at the door and slips into a pair of slippers or soft shoes.

PREPARING BEDS

Members are allowed to use their own sleeping bag, down or synthetic filled, provided a sheet sleeping bag is used along with it. As blankets are provided in the hostels it is easier to use only a sheet sleeping bag. These are designed in such a manner that the hosteller does not come into contact with the blankets or the pillow. A pocket is provided in the sheet into which the pillow slips, and there is a flap big enough to go over the top of the blankets. It is in the interests of all that sheet sleeping bags should be clean and tidy and in good condition. A freshly laundered sheet sleeping bag can be hired for a small charge at most hostels.

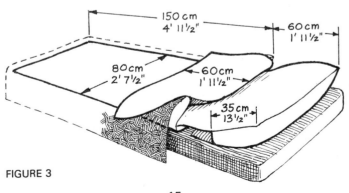

FIGURE 3

COOKING

When self cooking, bear in mind that others will want to use the facilities after you, so remember to wash and dry all pots and crockery as soon as you are finished using them. Tables should also be wiped down before you leave the kitchen. Depending on the hostel, cooking should be completed before 10 p.m. (22.00 hours) or half-an-hour before the hostel closing time.

CLOSING TIME

Depending on the hostel, and the country where you are hostelling, you should be in bed, with the lights out, by the stated closing time. Silence must usually be observed until 7 a.m. Many hostellers spend long hours during the day walking or cycling, and do not appreciate being kept awake by noisy dormitory companions. Consider others and if someone is sleeping in your dorm, no matter what time it is, keep as quiet as possible.

DEPARTURE

After you have completed your hostel duty, immediately prior to departure, membership cards should be collected from the warden.

DAY CLOSING

As youth hostels are provided to encourage people to visit the countryside and places of cultural interest, they close down during the day. Again it depends on which country you are visiting, or which grade of hostel you are staying at. Many hostels close at different times and for different durations. Generally though the closing time is from 10 a.m. to 5 p.m. or thereabouts, but there are some hostels in Scotland which only close from 11 a.m. to 2 p.m. Again it pays dividends to consult the handbook of the country you are visiting.

ANIMALS

Animals are not allowed in hostels.

FIRE DANGER

Fires are not allowed to be lit within the hostel grounds. On occasions, permission may be given to hold a barbecue outside the hostel, but under such circumstances the warden will be in attendance and in charge. Petrol must not be brought within fifteen feet of a hostel building, and motor vehicles should be parked as directed by the warden.

BEHAVIOUR

Smoking is banned in dormitories. This is an obvious follow-on from the last heading, and must not, under any circumstances, be disobeyed. A fire in a youth hostel could have horrific results and an absolute awareness of fire risk is vital.

Gambling, and the use of drugs and alcohol are prohibited. Anyone who appears at a hostel under the influence of drink or drugs will be refused admittance. Radios, tape recorders and musical instruments may be played in the common room only. It is only good manners to ask anyone in the common room if they have any objection to you playing music or a radio. In most cases a musical instrument can lead to an entertaining evening, often turning into an impromptu folk-concert. As in all other aspects of youth hostelling, common sense will tell you how to behave in a manner befiting decent hostellers. If you remember you are sharing the hostel with people just like yourself, you won't go far wrong.

RESPONSIBILITIES

Members are personally responsible for any damage they may cause to property belonging to the Youth Hostel and for their own luggage and equipment. The Hostel Association is not responsible for the safety of members property within the hostel. The warden in charge is not bound to accept articles handed to him for safe keeping. If he does, such articles remain at the member's risk. Always keep articles of value on your person. Theft is a rare occurrence in a youth hostel but the less chance for possible temptation to a thief the better. Although cycle accommodation is nearly always available, you are advised to personally insure your bike as the hostel cannot be held responsible for any theft or damage that may occur. In the event of any article going missing advise the warden immediately.

INFECTION

Naturally, no one who is suffering from, or has been in contact with, an infectious disease is allowed to use a hostel.

AGE LIMITS

Despite the name, people of any age can use youth hostels, provided they are over the age of five. Exceptions to this rule are in the case of hostels providing family accommodation, where children under five can stay provided they are using the family accommodation with their parents. In parts of Germany there is an upper age limit of 27, and in Switzerland priority is given to people under the age of 25.

Hostellers are expected to behave in a decent and well behaved manner during their stay at a Youth Hostel. It is one of the warden's duties to report breaches of discipline to the proper quarter. In the case of a serious offence, membership cards will be withheld pending official enquiry. As I said at the beginning, the rules have been made by other hostellers. In general, unpleasantness is rare, so come hostelling, observe the rules, and enjoy yourself.

Chapter 3

WHERE ARE THE HOSTELS?

Let's take another look at the main aim and ideal of the youth hostel movement. *'To help all, but particularly young people to know, use, and appreciate the countryside and places of historic and cultural interest, by providing simple hostel accommodation for them on their travels.'*

The countryside, places of historic and cultural interest covers pretty well an immense area, not only in Britain and Ireland, but also in 48 other countries all over the world.

IN BRITAIN AND IRELAND

In England and Wales there are over 250 hostels, Scotland has 80, Northern Ireland has 12, and the An Oige Association in Eire has 47.

Although it is tempting to buy a membership card and head off across the Channel to sample hostelling abroad, it is a good idea to do some previous touring in this country. This will give you a good idea of the traditions of hostelling, and will provide such experience without the additional complications of language and currency.

CITY HOSTELS

Before sitting down and working out a tour, you will have to decide where you want to go. If you are not an outdoor type, and prefer ambling around old churches or museums, do not despair; you are well catered for in some of the city hostels, and hostels situated in or near the historic centres. London has four hostels, so if you like the idea of visiting the famous tourist spots like St. Paul's Cathedral, the Houses of Parliament, Buckingham Palace, or the Tower of London, then off you go. Edinburgh, Dublin and Belfast all have hostels, as do Glasgow, Newcastle and Norwich. As well as offering much interest in the way of old buildings and museums, these cities are also good stopping off points en route to the marvellous country that surrounds them. Take a train or bus from home, stay a night in the city hostel, and then take off for the delights of the countryside come the morning.

COUNTRY HOSTELS

It is in the country that Youth Hostelling comes into its own. Unless you are camping, it is not always easy to find

FIGURE 4

FIGURE 5

21

accommodation where you are out in the wilds. There are even hostels in completely desolate areas, like Loch Ossian, and Glen Affric in Scotland, where you are surrounded by nothing but mountains, lochs, and breathtaking scenery. There are 30 hostels in the Lake District, ranging from large busy ones like Ambleside, and the purpose-built one at Patterdale, to the peace and solitude of Black Sail and Coniston. North Wales is also a popular area, especially for climbers and hill-walkers, and again, a plethora of hostels make good trips possible.

In Northern Ireland and Eire, small, simple hostels are the main attractions, and they are increasingly becoming popular as 'escape' hostels. Even the names sound romantic and relaxing; Glendaloch, Aghavannagh, Black Valley, Ben Lettery and Errigal; or how about Allihies, Currane, or Killary Harbour. Names that conjure up images of folklore, fiddle music, the leprechauns and the Banchee, and long peaceful evenings trout fishing in one of Irelands fine rivers.

LONG-DISTANCE FOOTPATHS

If you are a keen walker, try some of the long distance footpaths. The Pennine Way, for example, has hostel accommodation along its entire length, beginning at Edale in Derbyshire, and passing the vicinity of another 22 before finishing in Scotland at Kirk Yetholm Hostel.

UNUSUAL HOSTELS

Some of the hostels themselves are well worth a visit in their own right. Carbisdale Castle in the north of Scotland is a genuine castle of immense and breathtaking proportion, and has still, adorning its halls and walls, the same paintings and statues with which it was originally equipped. The converted barge, The Sabrina, at Selby in North Yorkshire, is one of the most unusual, and boasts the title of Britain's only floating Youth Hostel. Castles, mansions, cottages, a shepherds hut, farm buildings, a water mill and a Norman keep are all typical of the type and variety of buildings used as Youth Hostels.

PLANNING A TRIP

There is so much to see in Britain and Ireland that you could not possibly hope to cover it all in one trip. That may sound a bit obvious, but every year, tourists do attempt to 'do' Britain in a week, and generally they go home rather discontented after seven days of sitting in a car or train. All they really see of the

DALES WAY

CLEVELAND WAY

WOLDS WAY

PENNINE WAY

CAMBRIAN WAY

OFFAS DYKE PATH

EAST ANGLIAN WAY

PEMBROKE COAST PATH

COTSWOLD WAY

RIDGEWAY PATH

NORTH DOWNS WAY

SOUTH DOWNS WAY

SOUTH WEST PENINSULA COAST PATH

FIGURE 6

23

country is the inside of railway stations, or their hostel dormitory at night.

Although the various Hostel Associations have tried hard to provide hostels in all the areas of outstanding beauty or interest, there may be some gaps, so you should plan your trip carefully, and take this fact into consideration.

The Association handbooks, available from any headquarters are an invaluable help in trip planning. They list all the hostels, their opening and closing times, their exact situation, facilities available, and the local attractions within the reach of the hostel. Maps, with distances shown between the hostels, are also included.

BOOKING IN ADVANCE

In the more popular areas, such as the Lake District, or the Scottish Highlands, and especially during the busy periods like July and August, you are strongly advised to book in advance. A 'Hostel Full' sign is not uncommon during the summer. Although the warden is always reluctant to turn someone away, the Fire Regulations make it difficult for him to accommodate more people than his hostel caters for.

Plan well in advance. If you think the hostel may be busy, write to the warden and reserve a bed, saying when you expect to arrive, when you will depart, how many people you are booking for, male and female, and remember to enclose a stamped addressed reply envelope. For your first trip you are better to book in advance at all the hostels you want to visit, but after a bit of experience, you will learn which hostels require booking and which ones don't.

Chapter 4

GOING ABROAD

Once you have sampled hostelling in this country and have a good idea what it is all about, you may well want to further your horizons and go off on a trip abroad. Over 4,000 hostels in nearly 50 countries give you a good choice, and your Hostel Membership card, by international agreement admits you to all of them.

INTERNATIONAL YOUTH HOSTEL FEDERATION
The various national Youth Hostel Associations are linked together in the International Youth Hostel Federation, the aim of which is to facilitate international travel and understanding among young people of the world. The basic rules are the same in every country. As in Britain and Ireland, each hostel is managed by a warden, or houseparent as they are called on the Continent, who will help you in every way possible to have an enjoyable holiday.

MEMBER COUNTRIES
Countries belonging to the I.Y.H.F. are: Argentine, Australia, Austria, Belgium, Bulgaria, Canada, Cyprus, Czechoslovakia, Denmark, Egypt, Finland, France, West Germany, Greece, Holland, Hungary, Iceland, India, Northern Ireland, Eire, Israel, Italy, Japan, Kenya, Korea, Lebanon, Luxembourg, Malaysia, Morocco, New Zealand, Norway, Pakistan, Philippines, Poland, Portugal, Scotland, Spain, England and Wales, Sri Lanka, Sweden, Switzerland, Syria, Thailand, Tunisia, U.S.A., Uruguay, and Yugoslavia.

PASSPORTS
Passports are required for all countries outside Great Britain and Ireland. There are two types; (1) One which currently costs £10 and which is valid for ten years. Application forms for this type are obtainable from any Post Office or your local passport office. (You'll find the address in your telephone directory.) Apply for this passport at least three weeks before your date of departure. (2) The second kind is available only from main Post Offices. It costs £5, and is valid for 12 months. This is the British Visitors Passport and its validity is limited to Western Europe, Canada, the Canary Islands, Madiera, Bermuda, and the Azores.

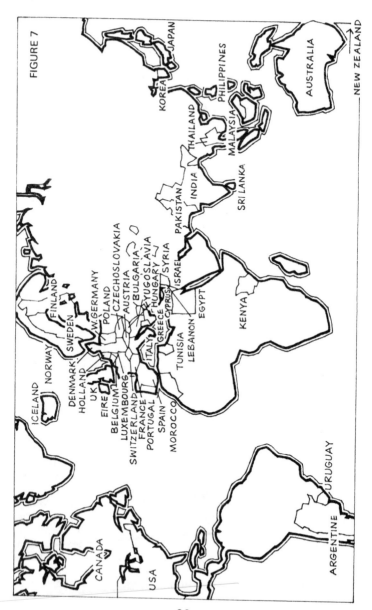

FIGURE 7

26

MEDICAL SERVICES

Visitors to countries in the common market can avail themselves of medical services on the same basis as the nationals of the country they are visiting, provided they obtain the appropriate certificate of entitlement from the Department of Health and Social Security before leaving Britain. Certain other countries in Europe have reciprocal arrangements, information about which can be obtained from the Home Office or Social Security Department Offices.

INSURANCE

To cover all eventualities, you should insure against medical expenses, personal accident, loss or theft of personal effects, etc.

MONEY

Take enough foreign money for the first few days of your holiday, and change the rest of your cash into travellers cheques. You can purchase both the foreign currency and the travellers cheques at a bank.

AGE LIMITS

Children under 14 years of age may not use Youth Hostels outside their own country unless they are accompanied by an adult relative of the same sex, or, by a group leader holding a Leader Card. A minimum age of five years is observed in most countries. Most associations generally give priority to younger members, and wardens are in fact entitled to refuse bookings from members over 30 if such bookings would result in the exclusion of younger members.

BOOKINGS

Advanced booking is advised in July and August, and during most periods of the year at city hostels and hostels in popular tourist areas. You should write to the hostel concerned, using an International Booking Form which are available from any Youth Hostel Office. Enclose an International Reply Coupon (available from Post Offices) for the Warden's reply.

THE LANGUAGE BARRIER

Language is not a total barrier. In many countries English is spoken as a second language by the majority of locals, especially among the younger people, but it is very useful, as well as polite,

FIGURE 8

28

to be able to communicate in the local language. It is surprising how well you can manage with very little practice, and long conversations can be had with only the knowledge of a few basic phrases.

USEFUL PHRASES

Without attempting to write a foreign-phrase book, I have listed some words that should help you get by, and may even help you enjoy your holiday that little bit more.

General phrases — English, French and German are the most used languages in Europe, so I have given the phrase first in English, then in French and German.

At the Airport —
Airport Terminal — L'aerogare — Flughaven
Luggage Registration — L'enregistrement des baggages — Die Gepäckaufgabe.
Flight Number — Le numero de vol — die Flugnummer.
Delay — retard — die Verspätung.
Duty Free shop — la boutique hors-taxes — zollfreier Verkaufsstand.

At the Customs —
Customs Office — le bureau de douane — des Zollant
Passport — le passport — der (Reise) pass.
Have you anything to declare? — avez vous quelque chose a declarer? — Haben Sieetwas zu verzollen?
Foreign Currency — l'argent etranger — die ausländische Währung.

In the Youth Hostel —
Wardens Office — le bureau de P. A. (PAY-AH) — die Anmeldung.
The Kitchen — La cuisine — Die Küche.
Dormitory — le dortior — Der Schlafraum
Membership Card — la carte — der Herbergsausweis.
Have you room for me? — avez vous encore une place pour moi? — haben Sie noch Platz fur mich.
What is my duty? — quelle est ma corvée? — welche Arbeit soll ich tun?

Making Friends —
What's your name? — comment vous' appellez-vous? — wie heissen Sie?
Please write down your address — donne moi votre adresse s'il vous plait — bitte, schreiben Sie Ihre Adresse auf.

FIGURE 9

Hitch Hiking —
Can you give me a lift to — pouvez-vous m'emmener jusqu'a —
Können Sie mich nach (destination) mitnehmen.

These few words should help you to get about during the first few days of your holiday abroad, but really, lack of language is no barrier to simple friendly communication. Strictly speaking hitch-hiking is forbidden or frowned upon in many Continental countries.

Chapter 5

COURSES AND HOLIDAYS

Although Youth Hostels are provided primarily for those who are travelling in the U.K., both the English and the Scottish Associations arrange an extensive programme of holidays and courses. These courses are ideally suited for those who want to try something different, and the Scottish Youth Hostels Association even arranged a holiday on which you can try a wide range of outdoor sports from grass-skiing to archery, all in the space of one week.

One thing that all the courses have in common is that they will give you a thorough introduction to the activity of your choice, under expert instruction, and for those with some experience already, many advanced courses are held throughout the year.

HILL WALKING AND MOUNTAINEERING

Walking and climbing seem to be the most popular outdoor activities, and these courses are held in centres throughout the country, from the relatively gentle terrain of the Suffolk Coast or the Malverns and Wye Valley, to rock climbing in the Cuillins of Skye or mountaineering in the Cairngorms. It is advised that all applicants for walking or climbing courses wear vibram-soled boots, and, to save discomfort and a possible quick exit from the course boots should be well broken in and the feet hardened before arrival at the start. The correct warm and windproof clothing should be bought or hired.

FIGURE 10

FIGURE 11

WATER SPORTS

Canoeing and Sailing are also popular activities. Locations range from Loch Lomond and Loch Lochy in Scotland to river canoeing in England and sailing on Welsh lakes. It is a condition on all sailing and canoeing courses that applicants can swim at least 50 yards wearing light clothing. Life jackets, which must be worn at all times on the water, are normally supplied to participants.

Still on the water, or at least under it, underwater swimming is organised at Salcombe in Devon. Instructors from the British Sub-Aqua Club will take you progressively from your first underwater session, to aqua-lung diving, taking a look at various diving sites and underwater wrecks. For this course you must be able to swim at least 200 yards.

33

PONY TREKKING

Pony trekking is always a favourite with the girls, and the Border country, with its history of border feuds and well supplied with old drove roads is first class for trekking. For the advanced trekker an extensive tour is arranged from Capel-y-ffin Youth Hostel in Wales, covering the bridleways and country lanes of the Black Mountains and the Brecon Beacons. Overnight stops are made at hostels and guest houses in the area. Dartmoor also gives good trekking over the wild heather covered moorland, and this course is based at Tavistock Youth Hostel.

FIGURE 12

FIGURE 13

CYCLING

'Off the Beaten Track' cycling tours are arranged by the Scottish Youth Hostel Association in conjunction with the Cyclists Touring Club. Each tour lasts for a week and leaves behind the busy main roads for the quietness of forests and private, and secondary roads. Distances normally covered vary from thirty to sixty miles daily, and the tours are particularly suited to family groups and novices.

Other cycling tours are arranged in Yorkshire, the South Downs, Wales and Kent.

MISCELLANEOUS

More unusual pastimes are also catered for, ranging from Industrial Archaeology and Rural Crafts, to Mineral Collecting and Geology. Bird Watching is provided in the New Forest, and for those with an artistic inclination, painting, sketching and printmaking can be arranged at the peaceful Lakeland setting of Chapel House.

Although you must be a member of a Youth Hostel Association to participate in any of these courses, you don't necessarily have to be an experienced hosteller. In all courses and holidays there will always be someone around to show you the Hostelling 'ropes'.

Chapter 6

WHAT YOU'LL NEED

What kind of equipment you will need, and how much you will have to carry, depends very much on the type of trip you are planning. Many hostellers, especially those from abroad, are quite happy to spend most of the day sitting on a bus or train, just travelling from hostel to hostel around the country. If you were travelling like this, ordinary everyday clothing and a suitcase to carry your bits and pieces would suffice. If you intend travelling by car, then again, there is no need for any special gear, apart from specialist equipment if you had thoughts of doing some hill-walking or other activities like fishing, pony trekking, during the holiday. Although car borne hostellers are becoming more and more common, the majority of young people in the U.K. travel to hostels by means of the 'thumb'.

Hitch-hiking seems to have become an accepted mode of travel in recent years, and every summer the highways and byways of Britain and Ireland become dotted every few hundred yards by young folk clad in denim carrying the universal badge of itinerant youth, the pack-frame or rucksack. More about the pros and cons of hitch-hiking in the next chapter, but for now let us take a look at the equipment you will need to travel comfortably between overnight stops.

CLOTHING

First of all, what will you need to carry with you on a youth hostelling trip? Clothing can get quite wet and dirty when you have to walk any distance, especially beside a road, with the cars and lorries splashing dirt and mud on you every few minutes. Spare clothing is therefore essential. Although jeans are to be discouraged as hill walking wear, they are perfectly adequate for travelling. Denim is quite hard wearing, fashionable, and more often than not, comfortable. Most hostels nowadays are equipped with drying rooms, so it is a good idea to dry, or even wash your travelling clothes every night, and wear them again next day, keeping your spare clothes clean and dry for wearing around the hostel in the evenings. Soft shoes are an essential part of the kit, as outdoor shoes, and in particular, Vibram-soled boots are not allowed in the hostel. Slippers make idea hostel wear, as they are light and comfortable and easily crammed inside a pack.

FIGURE 14

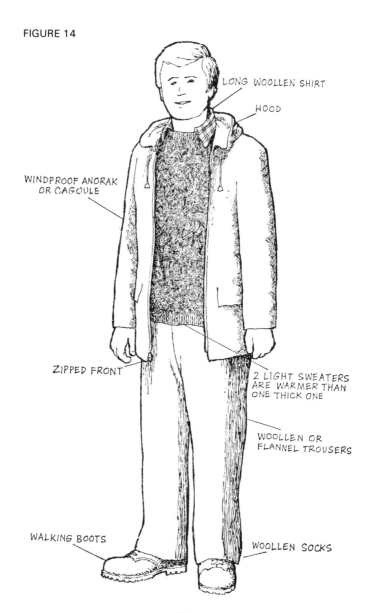

LONG WOOLLEN SHIRT

HOOD

WINDPROOF ANORAK OR CAGOULE

ZIPPED FRONT

2 LIGHT SWEATERS ARE WARMER THAN ONE THICK ONE

WOOLLEN OR FLANNEL TROUSERS

WALKING BOOTS

WOOLLEN SOCKS

COOKING UTENSILS

Youth hostels in the U.K. are well equipped with pots, pans and crockery, but if you intend visiting hostels in Scotland and Ireland you will have to carry your own knife, fork and spoon. Many camping stores sell neat little knife fork and spoon sets which fold up together and take up very little space. Fold your cutlery in a tea towel, a useful item to have in the kitchen, especially when the hostel ones are all wet. This always seems to happen when the hostel is busy and the warden isn't about, so, bring your own and lessen the chances of being stuck with wet pots and pans. After your evening meal, hang your tea towel in the drying room with your travelling clothes, keeping it nice and dry for packing away next morning.

TOILET REQUISITES

Soap, towel, and other toiletries, are personal items that everyone, well, almost everyone, carries habitually. Night attire seems to vary greatly from person to person, and it is useful to have a small torch next to your pillow in case of a nocturnal trip to the lavatory.

SHEET SLEEPING BAGS

As I said in Chapter 2, a sheet sleeping bag is compulsory for hygiene reasons. A sheet sleeping bag weighs very little, but if you want to travel ultra-lightweight, you can usually hire one at the hostel on your arrival.

FIRST AID KIT

A first aid kit is a useful item to carry in your pack, especially if you are visiting a remote simple hostel. Also, you never know when you will come across an accident in the road, so it is as well to be prepared.

DOCUMENTS

Membership card, hostel handbook, and maps, more or less complete the kit. Many camping stores sell useful little money belts, which enable you to keep your personal documents and cash on your person at all times.

RAINWEAR

Waterproofs are an essential part of outdoor travelling whether you are walking, cycling, or hitch-hiking. To keep the rain out, you will need a nylon cagoule, or even better, a waterproof jacket with a front-opening zip. The main problem with cagoules is that the smock design tends to encourage condensation, whereas with a full-length zip down the front, the jacket can be opened at any time to allow air in to circulate, and cool down the body.

Although condensation is almost inevitable with nylon clothing, it can be controlled to a great extent by letting some air in to circulate every now and again, and the very light weight and compressability of nylon just cannot be ignored, especially on long trips when weight is an important point. Waterproof trousers are also an essential part of the kit, and they should preferably have a zip up the side to make them easy to put on and take off over boots. Coupled with your waterproof jacket and gaiters these will give you full protection and head to toe waterproofing.

HAT

Assuming that your jacket is fitted with a hood, it is not strictly necessary to wear a hat but in the colder months, a woollen balaclava can make a crucial difference to being warm or cold. It has been said that the human body can lose up to 35 per cent of its heat through the head, so wearing a hat is really a good method of temperature control, especially in winter.

FOOTWEAR

Boots or stout shoes make life more comfortable on the road, as walking for long periods in training shoes or fashion shoes can cause all kinds of problems from blisters to fallen arches. More about boots in Chapter 9.

PACKS

Now that you've collected all the bits and pieces together, you will need something to carry it all in. A small lightweight rucksack fits the bill perfectly. For the past few years, the High Pack, or the Frame Pack, has enjoyed an enormous amount of popularity, but unless you intend going off on a long journey, with a vast amount of gear, these large capacity packs are superfluous. Not only are they too big, but the frame can be a real nuisance to manhandle off and on buses, cars and trains. A large bulky pack can really spoil your chances of getting a lift if you are hitch hiking. Many

FIGURE 15

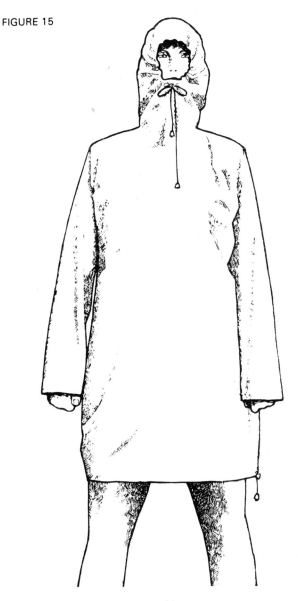

KARRIMOR BAMBAINO 2.   KARRIMOR TACPAC.

FIGURE 16

youth hostels I have visited recently show signs of clumsily
handled frames, in the form of badly scratched and dented floors
and walls. This is the result of hostellers using their pack as a
battering ram to open doors. Frame packs were designed for back
packers who have to carry big loads, including sleeping bags,
tents, stoves, and several days food, all items which are not
strictly necessary to carry on a hostelling trip, unless of course,
you intend mixing camping and hostelling on one journey.

TRAVEL LIGHT

A small nylon rucksack, of about thirty to forty litres capacity,
should be perfectly adequate for one or two weeks hostelling.
Berghaus, Karrimor and Vango all manufacture sacks in this
range, with either a small integral frame, or with no frame at all.
So, think lightweight, and travel between hostels comfortably
and with the minimum possible fuss. And, of course, no aching
shoulders.

Chapter 7

HITCH HIKING

Hitch hiking can be defined as travelling by begging lifts from passing motorists. A few years ago the population at large tended to frown upon hitch hikers as anti-social hippies and drop outs, but today it is widely accepted by most people. In many cases it is by travelling on "the thumb" that enables young people, especially students, to have a holiday at all. Combined with youth hostelling it makes a very cheap method of seeing the country, and it is common practice nowadays for people to hitch hike all over the world, although it is sometimes illegal, and sometimes dangerous — both for hitch hiker *and* motorist.

SIMPLE RULES
Occasionally however quite apart from the foreseen risk, someone does something stupid, and all hitch hikers tend to suffer as a result of the publicity. It is important to remember a few simple rules, that will not only make life a bit easier for you, but will leave drivers with a good impression and will encourage them to stop their cars for hitch hikers again.

TECHNIQUE
Speaking as a driver, there is nothing that annoys me more than seeing young people lounging on the grass at the side of the road with their thumb stuck up in the air. If you want a lift, make it look as if you are in fact going somewhere. Although you are in theory begging for a lift, try not to make it look like that. Look smart and alert, make an attempt at walking along the side of the road, and wave you thumb positively. Glance around as the car approaches and try and look cheerful. A driver will not stop if he thinks he is going to get stuck with a miserable, bored individual who looks as though the world is about to come to an end. Lorry drivers in particular look for a bit of lively company, especially when they have to drive for long hours on their own. If you look as though you will make good company for a while, then your chances of a lift will increase.

MOTORWAYS
It against the law in this country and on European autobahns for pedestrians to walk on the hard shoulder of a motorway. If you must wait at the entrance to a motorway, use a placard with your

destination printed in large clear letters. It is also good practice to add the word *'Please'* after the name of the town. During peak periods, in summer and during university vacations, motorway entrances become rather crowded with hitch hikers. Walk back down the road a little way and try your hitching from there. The chances are that others will try the same thing, but that is all part of the game, and this is when ingenuity and gamesmanship will play their part.

POOR TECHNIQUES

One technique which does not often pay off is when one hitch hiker stands at the roadside hitching, while his friends hide behind a tree or hedge! The unsuspecting driver comes along, decides to give the poor solitary hiker a lift, and before he knows what has happened, his car is besieged by another two or three. This is the kind of trick that puts people off hitch hikers. More often than not the tricksters find themselves left behind at the side of the road in a cloud of dust, often with some sharp words ringing in their ears, and rightly so.

Another unfair trick is to hide a really immense pack behind the wall, and then start hitching with only a small handbag or day sack. It always seems to be the drivers of small cars who stop on these occasions or drivers with their family in the back. You can imagine their consternation when this huge rucksack is pulled out of hiding, all ready to be stuffed in through the rear window.

LUGGAGE

As a follow-on from this point, try and pare your luggage down to a bare minimum. Guitars, extra hand luggage, massive pack frames, which often damage car interiors, and in general, excessive baggage, can all stop drivers from stopping, usually because the driver simply has no room for you and your luggage.

APPEARANCE

This is an important point. Although beards and long hair are pretty well accepted nowadays, dirty or way-out clothes are not. Keep it in mind that a driver will not really get a good look at you as he approaches, and his very first impression will decide him whether to stop or not. If that first impression tells him that some dirty hobo looks as though he wants a lift, the chances are that he will drive on past wondering what todays youth is coming to. On the other hand, if he glimpses a clean looking, well-turned-out youngster, with a cheerful smile as he waves his thumb, then the chances of the motorist stopping to pick up this smart young fellow are so much better.

WHEN A CAR STOPS

If you are in luck and somebody stops for you, don't amble over slowly and ask the driver where he is going, as if you couldn't really care less. When the vehicle stops, pick up your gear and run to it. The driver may be in a hurry. Bid the driver good day, in his own language if you are abroad, and tell him where you are heading. He will then tell you if he can take you there, or perhaps he will tell you he can only take you part of the way. If this is the case, accept the lift anyway, with thanks, and at least you will be part of the way to reaching your destination.

IN THE CAR

Drivers don't as a rule pick up hitch hikers because they want to carry an extra load. They pick up hitchers because they may be bored with their journey, or want a good chat with someone; because you may look like an interesting person to meet, or because they feel sorry for you because they were young once themselves. Open up a conversation immediately. Be polite but chatty. At road junctions tell him whether your side of the road is clear or not. In general try and be good company. Refrain from smoking, unless invited to do so; don't turn down windows unless invited to do so; don't criticise his driving, unless it is very obviously dangerous and you fear for your safety in which case get out; tampering with the radio, or controls will be an irritation. When you are dropped off at your destination, wish your driver goodbye and good luck with his journey. Make him feel as though he has done you an immense favour. If you go about your hitching properly, the drivers who give you a lift will probably stop for another hitch hiker another day; and you never know, that hitcher may be you again.

DANGERS

Unfortunately, hitch hiking has its dangers, and to cut these to a minimum, do not hitch alone. There is no doubt that solo hitch-hiking is the easiest way to get a lift, but lone hikers, especially girls, are an instant attraction to the stranger members of society. Boy and girl is the best combination for a hitch hiking partnership, and will travel safely and quickly. Two boys may have some difficulty especially if they look at all rough, but two girls should manage very well. There is only one rule about girls travelling alone and that is DON'T. There are many potential wolves frequenting our highways and byways. At best you will come across some amourous Casanova, eager to try out his "chatting-up" techniques. At the very worst? Well, the press is usually full of it, and the details are not very pleasant. If you think that someone is about to pull a fast one on you, ask him politely to stop the car as you feel sick. Another trick is to wait until you see another hitch-hiker and then ask him to stop as you have spotted a friend. If he does not stop, pretend you are going to be sick all over his upholstery. If that does not work, you are in trouble, so prepare yourself for some drastic action. Grab the ignition key, pull it out, and throw it away. Pretty drastic, I admit, but the chances of you getting into this position are rather remote, *unless you are on your own of course.*

Hitch hiking is like any other outdoor activity and calls for common sense. You may hit a stretch where nothing will stop for you, but keep on persevering. I have never yet heard of a hitch hiker who has not reached his destination.

Finally, an important point. If you are a juvenile, ask your parents if you may hitch hike. If they won't allow it, don't. If they do, be careful, and good hitching to you.

Chapter 8

CYCLE TOURING

Because of the basic simplicity of the two pastimes, cycle touring and hostelling have a special affinity for each other. The cheap, simple accommodation in the company of kindred souls is a good way to end a long day in the saddle. The thought of a huge meal, a shower, and an evening in good company drives you onwards over the last few miles to the hostel.

POPULARITY

Cycle touring seems to have gained a second wind in this country. Immensely popular in pre-War days, when the youth hostels were bursting at the seams with cyclists every weekend, it seemed to die out a little with the advent of the motor car becoming, *'Not so much a Luxury, more a way of life.'* Whether the present population of Britain appreciate the benefits of regular exercise even in a mild form, or the concrete jungles of our cities are forcing more people into the countryside for their recreation, it is a fact that walking and cycling are two of the fastest growing sports in this country. When you consider the fact that over 30,000 cycle pannier bags were sold in this country last year it will give you a fair idea of the number of people who are turning to cycle touring as their own particular means of escape.

ADVANTAGES

Cycling is possibly the finest way of travelling between youth hostels. You don't have the hassle of bus or train time tables, there is no worry as to whether someone will be in such a benevolent mood that he will stop his car and give you a lift; it is relatively cheap; you are not affected by a fuel crisis; nor do you cause pollution. The bikes' ability to cover ground quite fast gives the tourer an opportunity to see a greater variety of countryside, and the larger distances between some of the hostels is much less of a problem than it is to the walker. Depending on your own physical condition, anything between 40 and 100 miles a day is possible, bringing most areas of Britain and Ireland well within the scope of your wheels.

TRAVELLING LIGHT

As with hiking, Travelling Light must also be the criterion of the cyclist. The 'bikies' should be able to freewheel along the highways and byways with as little effort as possible. Heavy unbalanced loads prevent this, and merely cause frustration at the lack of smooth progress.

GEAR

All the items I mentioned in Chapter 6 can be carried on the bike, plus some bits and pieces of specialist gear which are necessary to keep both rider and machine churning along mile after mile. First of all, let us consider what makes the basis of a good touring bike.

THE BIKE

A strong, light, frame is essential. Strength, metal characteristics and design influence speed, acceleration, and comfort, subtly and positively. Total weight should be as little as possible. Every ounce counts, and perhaps suprisingly, lightweight components tend to be better made than their heavier counterparts. Fast-moving and wide ratio gears are the best, as most cyclists abhor the idea of having to dismount and push when ever there is a steep hill. The idea should be to keep on cycling, however slowly, and avoid the embarrassment of pushing a fully laden bike uphill. This calls for very low bottom gears. The emphasis should then be on a leisurely progress made possible without discomfort by adequate gearing.

Steel wheel rims are stronger than the cheaper alloy ones, and are more suited to riding over rough road conditions with a fully laden bike.

Although there are some very good plastic saddles now on the market, a good well broken-in leather one takes a lot of beating. Saddles should be ridden in over many miles of cycling, rather like walking boots, so don't discard a saddle too soon, if it appears to be rather uncomfortable after only a few miles. Another good buy, and a fair compromise in terms of price and comfort, is a padded nylon saddle covered with pile or suede.

Some tourers I know resolutely refuse to use dropped handlebars, perhaps unconsciously associating them with racing. The main purpose of such bars is to provide as many alternative hand positions for the long distance pedeller as possible, in an attempt to overcome the aches and pains caused by holding one position for a long period.

Good brakes on a touring bike are vital, as they have to act quickly on a fully laden bike under all weather conditions. Centre

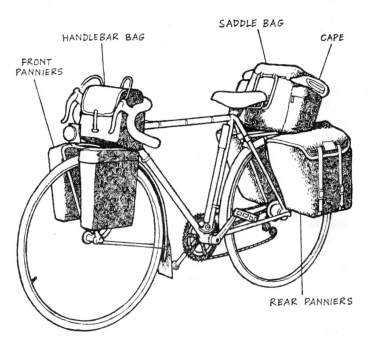

FRONT PANNIERS

HANDLEBAR BAG

SADDLE BAG

CAPE

REAR PANNIERS

SOME OF THE WAYS OF
CARRYING GEAR ON A CYCLE.

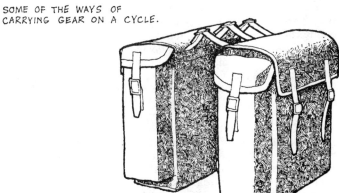

Y.H.A. 'SPECIAL' PANNIERS

FIGURE 17

49

pull brakes are most popular among experienced tourers with the levers for the brakes mounted at the bottom of the dropped handlebars.

BIKE BAGS

Having kitted yourself out with a reasonably good bike, the next important thing to consider is how to carry all your gear for a few days hostelling, safely and comfortably. For long distance touring, bags that attach to the bike are far preferable to rucksacks, which can chafe, impede circulation, strain the arms and back, block over-the-shoulder vision, and upset balance and riding efficiency by throwing the body out of the static position that maximises pedalling efficiency. There are three main categories of bike bag.

PANNIERS

Panniers are double bags which are supported on either side of the wheel by a rigid frame. Rear panniers are the basic bulk carrying bags used in bike touring. They should be well fitted to a rack which is bolted to the frame below the saddle, and must not in any way interfere with the wheels, the derailleur gear, or your feet. If the bags are deep enough to reach your feet they should be tapered to allow adequate clearance, as the pedals turn.

Front panniers tend to be a controversial issue. Some dislike them because they claim they encourage overweighting the front wheel and cause steering problems, while others feel that they counterbalance heavy stern loads. Some special points to note when buying panniers include designs that allow them to be removed as double duty as hand luggage; drawstring closures that keep the bag taut on the bike; extra pockets; attaching points for securing loose gear, and inside compartments for organised packing.

HANDLEBAR BAGS

If you do not like the idea of front panniers, then consider the benefits of a handlebar bag. These bags provide the most accessible storage area for the cyclist, and are ideal for carrying such items as maps, cameras, hostel handbooks, and your lunchtime snack. You will find your handlebar bag works best if the top closure opens away from you, so you can see inside it quite easily while riding without having to rummage about blindly. A transparent, non-glare map case on top of the bag is very useful for quick map references.

STUFF SACKS

Rear panniers and a handlebar bag should be perfectly adequate storage space for any hostelling bikie, but if you think you will need some more packing space, then a large nylon stuff sack, strapped across the top of the panniers will serve this purpose admirably.

PACKING

As the balance of a touring bike is quite crucial, it is important to load your bags with the heavy items *as low and as close to the bike as possible*. This will help achieve a good load distribution and keep the bike stable on the road.

FIGURE 18

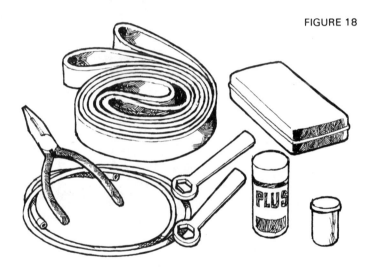

TOOLS

Enough tools should be included as part of the kit to enable running repairs to be made during the trip. The amount of spare parts that you carry with you depends on the length and whereabouts of the trip. It is a good idea to carry spare inner tubes, a set of tyre levers, a puncture repair kit, a spare derailleur cable and brake cable, some spare oil, a tube of grease, and a pair of pliers.

FIGURE 19

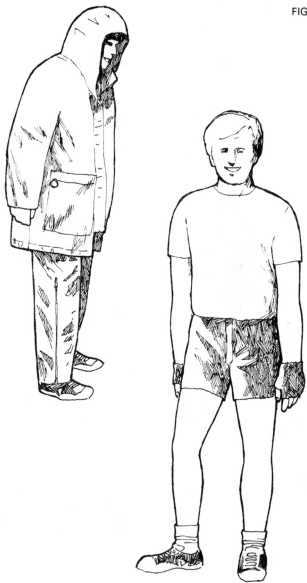

CLOTHING

As far as clothing is concerned, the main item is a good set of waterproofs. Make sure any rain gear you buy fits well, and also check that it fits your bike. Be sure that the jacket or more important, the trousers, won't interfere in any way with pedalling or steering. Capes or ponchos, once standard bikie wear, seems to have lost favour with todays tourers and two piece rain suits, always made in nylon, are now standard wear. The main point to remember is to buy rainwear in a suitably bright colour, day glo orange being, the best so that you will stand out *vividly* in traffic.

Shorts are ideal for summer use, with a pair of track suit trousers in the pack for the chillier hours. Breeches and long stockings are also popular, and are ideal for winter touring.

On the body, the tourer wears a string vest with a wool or acrylic vest over the top. In summer when the weather is warmer, a tee-shirt is adequate, keeping the body cool and protected from the sun. It is also a good idea to protect your hands in some way when cycling. There is nothing better than a good pair of fingerless mitts, such as those which racing cyclists wear.

Cycling shoes are specially designed for long hours of pedalling, but remember not to wear the kind with the metal bar on the sole, inside the hostel.

Cycle tourers are amongst the most independent of travellers with a special sense of freedom and a real chance to appreciate the countryside as they travel along. It is a marvellous way of travelling between hostels, and one that should be encouraged in every way, in this machine-crazy, car dependent, society of ours. The bike is probably the ultimate in self propelled non polluting travel, so give it a try. After the initial saddle soreness wears off you'll be a convert.

FIGURE 20

Chapter 9

HILL WALKING

It is no coincidence that most of Britain and Ireland's Youth Hostels are situated in or near mountain areas. We are very lucky in this country in that we have such wild areas reasonably close to our cities. When you consider the relatively cheap cost of transport to these areas, plus the low cost of youth hostelling, hill-walking holidays are within the purse strings of most. There is no valid reason why the hills of Wales, the Lake District and even the Scottish Highlands should not come within your compass. With a bit of experience, trips of several days duration can be taken from hostel to hostel, travelling over the hills and passes, far away from the bustle and grime of our busy roads. Energetic young men and women who have a predilection for hill country will find plenty of scope for their activities within the youth hostel network, and one of the great joys of hostelling is to spend a quiet evening by the fire after a hard days walking in the hills, in the company of others who also enjoy the peace and tranquility of the mountains.

SAFETY

Unfortunately, more and more people seem intent on courting disaster by going into the mountains unprepared both physically and mentally. The high tops of Wales, the Lakes, and in particular the Scottish Highlands, are no place for the absolute beginner, unless he or she is accompanied by an experienced walker. While there are always a few objective dangers lurking in the hills, most accidents are caused by some form of carelessness on the part of the walker involved. So *learn thoroughly* the basic rules for safety in the hills and remember this; the most important item of gear you carry into the hills is perched on your shoulders between your ears. Use it well. Common sense must always prevail and plan your trips thoroughly with a firm leaning on the side of safety.

ROUTE PLANNING

Before leaving home, plan your route well, with the aid of the relevant Ordnance Survey topographic maps. Estimate the time you will be away, and work out how long it will take you to travel between hostels. This is calculated by using Naismiths Rule, which states that you should allow *for 3 miles per hour plus an*

Sheet no: 184:   Start: Farm 896401   Finish: Hill 912442   Mag variation: 8°

Start	Mag°	Finish	Distance	Time
896401	88°	Barn 909403	2Km	45 mins
909403	48°	Church 916411	1Km (by track)	20 mins
916411	Map	Church 925424	3Km.Rd./F.pth	45 mins
925424	Map	Tumulus 920432	1Km-uphill	30 mins
920432	326°	Hill 912442	1Km	20 mins
	TOTAL	DISTANCE	8Km (5 miles)	160 mins 2 hrs. 40 mins say: 3 hrs.

FIGURE 21

extra hour for each 2,000 ft. climbed. This rule is a rough guide and should be adjusted to take into consideration eventualities like poor underfoot conditions, heavy loads carried, and poor physical fitness.

ROUTE CARDS

Leave a route card behind with the hostel warden every morning, jotting down such information as the names and addresses of all the party, equipment carried, the exact route to be taken quoting grid references and compass bearings and height climbed, objective, and estimated time of return, or arrival at your destination. It is also a good idea to add at the bottom of the card possible escape routes which you may have to take in the eventuality of an accident or bad weather. When you arrive at the next hostel phone the warden with whom you left the route card immediately in case you forget, and let him know you have arrived safely at your destination. Failure to do this may well result in search and rescue parties being called out un-necessarily.

SOLO HILLWALKING

Think twice about going on to the hills on your own. Even if you are very experienced, the unexpected can happen quite suddenly. In remote regions you could quite conceivably sprain an ankle and as a result of minor injury lie helpless for days. Three is a safe minimum for travelling into the hills.

RESCUE

Find out where the nearest telephones are on your chosen route, and the location of the nearest Mountain Rescue posts. These pieces of information could be vital if one of your party becomes involved in an accident, and you have to run for help.

MAP AND COMPASS

Make sure you carry in your pack, or better still, in your pocket, a map and compass. Read and learn how to use them from *The Spur Book of Map and Compass*, also published in this series.

EMERGENCY GEAR

Carry also a good First-Aid kit, and survival gear. This includes spare clothing, spare food, torch, whistle, remembering that the International Distress Signal is six blasts or torch flashes, each blast or flash at ten second intervals, followed by a sixty second pause and then repeat. Carry an emergency bivvy bag, or a large poly-bag.

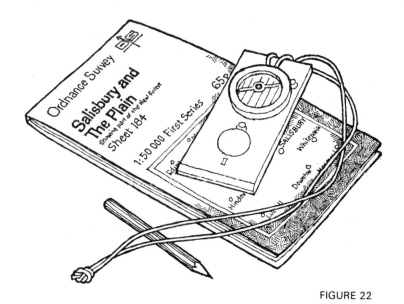

FIGURE 22

WEATHER CONDITIONS

Always keep an eye on the weather. Never be ashamed of having to give up or turn back if the weather turns nasty. The mountains will welcome you with open arms when the weather is fine, but when the Mountain Gods decide to let vent their anger in the form of wind and sleet, the hills make formidable opponents, even to the most experienced. Having said this, only experience can tell you when things are getting too rough, so don't run off the hill at the first hint of a dark cloud approaching. Remember what I said about using the head. Think well in advance, consider your capabilities, then act decisively. Good clothing will protect you to a certain extent from wind and rain, and there are certain other items which should be carried whenever you venture onto the hill.

CLOTHING

As with emergency gear, clothing should be checked, before departure *every day*. Woollen or thermal underwear is advised for the colder weather and string vests are popular in the summer months as the open mesh weave performs a double purpose. It

FIGURE 23

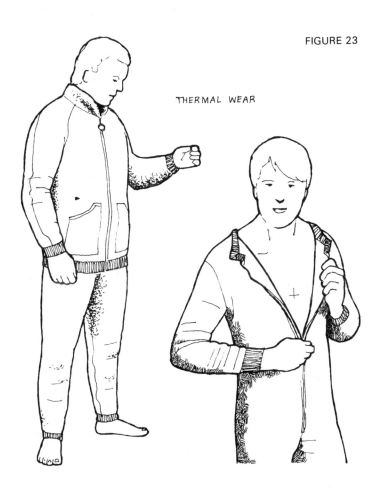

THERMAL WEAR

lets in cool air when exposed in the summer, and traps valuable body heat from escaping during colder weather. Breeches or trousers not jeans, should be worn. Although jeans are fine for hitch hiking and hostel wear, the thin material soaks up water like blotting paper and holds very little warmth. Jeans also tend to be rather tight fitting and so restrict leg movement.

Two or three woollen sweaters are better than one thick one, as body heat is trapped between the layers. The theory is simple, if you become too warm, take off a sweater. If you are still too warm, take off another, and vice versa when you get cold. Modern fibre pile garments like Helley Hansens' Polar suit makes good hill wear, the warmth being held in the fibre pile. A cotton bandage has a variety of uses, from a neck warmer, to an emergency sling, or even a sweat band.

RAINWEAR

Modern waterproof jackets have a dual purpose. They can be worn as a windproof, and waterproof shell. Buy one with a full length zipper up the front, and with a fitted hood.

CONDENSATION

As your active body gives off heat, the warm air travels through your clothing and hits the cool material of your waterproof jacket. As the jacket is proofed nylon, the warm air cannot pass through it, so like the steam from a boiling kettle hitting the cool kitchen window, the warm air condenses and water droplets form on the inside. Before very long you are wet inside, even though it might not even be raining. If you open the zip up every so often and let some cool air in to circulate, the warm air will be carried off and condensation eased. Waterproof trousers, which should also be carried, perform in much the same way.

HAT AND GLOVES

A woollen balaclava and gloves or mitts should always be carried in the hills, even in summer.

SOCKS

Finally, let's take a look at your feet. After all, its your feet that will act as a vehicle for carrying you over hill and dale for the duration of your holiday, so they deserve some very special attention. Two pairs of socks are better than one, for any friction inside the boot will be between the socks rather than between your foot and foot. Again, wool is best though nylon loop stitched socks are becoming quite popular. Carry a couple of spare pairs in your pack, and put on a clean pair every day. Dirty, sweaty socks insulate poorly and can cause blisters.

FIGURE 24

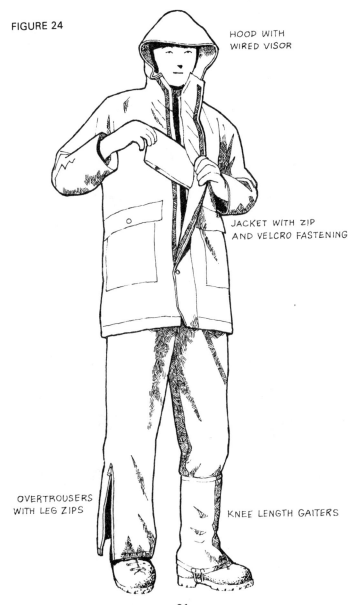

HOOD WITH
WIRED VISOR

JACKET WITH ZIP
AND VELCRO FASTENING

OVERTROUSERS
WITH LEG ZIPS

KNEE LENGTH GAITERS

BOOTS

Good boots are vital for a successful hill walk. These should be broad, comfortable and well-fitting. A sound rule to remember when buying your boots, is to push your foot as far into the boot as possible, so that your toes hit the end of the boot at the toecap. If the boots are the correct size, you should be able to insert a finger down the inside of the heel, and when you tighten the laces your foot should be held well into the back of the boot. The sole is the most important part of the boot, and the very best soles are of cleated rubber. These soles, being deeply patterned, give a good hold on dry rock earth. One word of warning however, such "Vibrams" do not grip well on snow, ice, wet grass, or wet rock. Be very careful how you go on these, and on hard snow or ice wear crampons, and carry an ice axe. Snow and ice climbing is out of the scope of this book, so if you have thoughts on winter mountaineering, read and learn as much as possible beforehand.

FIGURE 25

PACKS

Nylon rucksacks are very popular nowadays, but you should get into the habit of putting all your gear into the poly bag before putting it into the pack. When nylon packs are being manufactured, the holes made by the needles do not close over completely, and are therefore a prime source of water entry. Even though water does not get inside your pack, a poly bag will keep your gear nice and dry.

FINALLY

As you will have gathered from all this information youth hostelling is for some people an end in itself, while for others it is simply a means to an end, a way in which they can visit the countryside, using the hostel as a base. Whether you are a family group, a walker, a hill trekker, a back packer, a fisherman or whatever you will find a welcome at a youth hostel.

In return, all who use the countryside should appreciate that the green places are a shrinking commodity, under constant attack and increasing interference and control. Wildlife in particular suffers from the increasing use of the countryside for leisure, but even more from the ceaseless erosion of habitat.

The Country Code is a simple list of precepts for all country lovers so can I conclude by asking you to learn these rules and practise them.

THE COUNTRY CODE

Take care to avoid damaging farm property by remembering to:
1. Guard against all risks of fire.
2. Fasten all gates.
3. Keep dogs under proper control.
4. Keep to the paths across farmland.
5. Avoid damaging fences, hedges and walls.
6. Leave no litter.
7. Safeguard water supplies.
8. Protect wildlife, wild plants and trees.
9. Go carefully on country roads.
10. Respect the life of the countryside.